Mark McCauley, ASID

Color Therapy at Home

Real-Life Solutions for Adding Color to Your Life

GLOUCESTER MASSACHUSETTS

ROCKPORT PUBLISHERS

First published in the United States of America by
Rockport Publishers, Inc.
33 Commercial Street
Gloucester, Massachusetts 01930-5089
Telephone: (978) 282-9590
Facsimile: (978) 283-2742
www.rockpub.com

ISBN 1-56496-625-9

10 9 8 7 6 5 4 3 2 1

Cover Design: Chen Design Associates
Front and Back Cover Images: Architektur und Wohnen/Heiner Orth,
Jahreszeiten Verlag
Design: Cathy Kelley Graphic Design

Printed in China.

CONTENTS

INTRODUCTION

Our lives are forever shaped by, and inextricably bound to, the colors that surround us. Color moves us in ways both subtle and obvious; from the misty, muted pastels of the proverbial spring morning to the blaring reds of city traffic lights, color expands our emotions and helps direct our actions.

From the ancient to the present, man has ascribed certain powers to color. It can stimulate or depress, based on our collective associations with a particular hue. Primitive man understood color's therapeutic effect, utilizing its symbolism in early mystic rites. These cultures speak to us today, with color as their voice. The cave paintings at Alta Mira are alive with motion and depth through rudimentary pigments. The throne of Tutankhamen glows in gold raiment, counter pointed with the blue of lapis lazuli. The cries of dying Pompeii can be heard within interior walls coated in red and black. Color transcends time. It informs us of our past and thereby helps us to form our future.

Color has even greater significance when we harness its power within the home. Color is a shorthand used by society to communicate necessary information, as in the case of the traffic light. What would happen if we took this shorthand and applied it to our emotional, intellectual, and physical lives in our interior designs? For example, employing blue in a room to increase our sense of trust, for we associate honesty and trust with "true blue," as in the uniform of the policeman. Or perhaps yellow to replicate sunlight, as psychological studies indicate that virtually all children, when asked to draw the sun, color it yellow.

Would our lives become more meaningful if we arranged the colors in our homes as we arrange furniture, by first establishing a color's functionality with regard to our internal cognitive processes and physical needs before decorating? We can then answer these wants as we do with interior furnishings when deciding on the placement of sofas, chairs, dining tables, and beds. Does color provide physical clues to our environments? Can color serve as purveyor of intellectual thought, beyond its basic aesthetic qualities? Is it possible to enhance our emotional well-being through the use of color?

The answer is yes to all these questions. The proper arrangement of color in the home helps us on a physical level by serving as a signpost, i.e. defining a space as casual or formal, active, or passive. It promotes our intellectual life through clarity and impacts us emotionally when we combine colors for their psychological effect.

The first section of the book relates colors in terms of "associationism." In other words, how and why we associate a specific color with a given intellectual, emotional, or physical trait. For example, red is often thought of as dynamic. This comes from mankind's universal association of red with the color and movement of fire. Blue is seen as "cool," due to its association with water. Green is considered verdant, as it is associated with trees and plant life.

In the second half of the book, color is divided into categories that promote certain sets of complex human emotions, such as nurturing. Wishing to define a space as nurturing requires the incorporation of colors that we associate with this activity. These are delineated in the *Color Functions* section to help you create interiors that respond to your emotional needs. Color heals our emotional wounds. Unlocking the secrets of *Color Therapy* and applying them in the home brings release of our inner selves, and from this release springs a higher level of understanding. We become more in tune with the flow of our lives and share a higher communion with those who form such a large part of our lives; our families, friends, and loved ones.

Finally, The Color Choice Quiz on page 136 spells out the specific emotional, intellectual, and physical aspects of each color on the color wheel (and some "non-colors" such as black, white, and gray, which represent the addition or subtraction of light and are not found on the color wheel). Ascertain which you would like to promote in your life, and then, by referring to the Color Key on page 141, pick colors for your interiors that best reflect these desires.

By determining what colors work for you on these various levels, we begin the process of Color Therapy. By immersing ourselves in colors that provide the most emotional stability, we feel more serene and at peace. In our intellectual life, color provides impetus and serves our imaginations through fantasy. Physically, color denotes activity or passivity and heightens or diminishes spatial perception. Choosing colors that function best within these tripartite contexts allows us to place colors in the home to their greatest advantage for our mental, physical, and spiritual health.

Ultimately, we don't color our home, color *is* our home. Color impacts every waking second of our lives. Once we realize this simple fact, decorating the home with color takes on a whole new meaning. Color enhances our sense of self, our feelings of serenity within the home, and our relative happiness and contentment in general. As you adopt the principles in this book, I hope they bring you a long, colorful life.

Mark McCauley, ASID

COLOR

RED ORANGE GRAY PINK YELLOW BLUE BROWN WHITE GOLD

ASSOCIATIONS

PINK PINK RED PINK RED PINK RED PINK RED PINKRED PINK

RED/PINK

RED OUTRAGEOUS RED IS A HOT BUTTON. THE TURN-ME-ON IMMEDIACY OF

THE COLOR SIGNALS A CALL TO ACTION ON MANY LEVELS, FROM DANGER TO

COME HITHER. RED IS ROYAL AND RIGHTEOUS, RIFE WITH MEANING AND TIES

TO THE INTELLECT. IT BLUSHES OUR DEEPEST FEELINGS OF LOVE, SIGNIFYING

UNDYING PASSION AND INTIMACY. RED IS A ROSE, QUOTH THE BARD. YET, IN CON-

TRADICTION, RED IS MARS, THE GOD OF WAR, AND WAR IS HELL. RED IS THE YIN

AND THE YANG OF THE SPECTRUM, THE DR. JEYKLL AND MR. HYDE OF COLORS.

RED IS PREEMINENT AMONG THE PRIMARIES. HARNESSING THE

ENVIRONMENT, IT FINALLY SUBJUGATES OTHER HUES, LEAVING CRIMSON KING,

HIGHLY DEFINED AND INTREPID. ALL HAIL THE KING OF HEARTS AND MINDS,

RED REIGNS. FORCE, ENERGY, AND VIGOR ARE FOUND IN RED. IT INDICATES A

TORRID TEMPER, THE NERVOUS TURMOIL OF THE SOUL. DOMINEERING AND

QUICK TO ACT, RED IS A FIST THROUGH THE WALL. ROILING RED ASSAULTS THE

SENSES AND REFUSES TO YIELD. IT SPEAKS TO THE EGO, THE SELF-CENTERED

CHILD WITHIN WHO NEEDS IMMEDIATE GRATIFICATION.

above: This medieval checked pattern stresses royalty. The feeling of formality is heightened by the dark values of red alternating with lighter golden yellow, which adds a sense of intellectualism.

following page: "Love comes in at the eye," or so said William Butler Yeats. And it certainly does in this romantic harvest, where a variety of red elements (fabric, candle, and potpourri) are highlighted by glistening silver. The immediacy of love leaps from the scene to the consciousness when viewing this silken, damask-driven combination of red values.

Red empowers the individual. It gives us the strength and ability to be in and of the real and now. There is no backpedaling or tap dancing with this color. Here I am, says red, take me as you find me. The Ernest Hemingway of colors, red flies off, sails off, takes off for parts unknown and dangerous. Red doesn't listen, it decides. It is the color of action, instinctual and basic in emotion, love or hate. Patience is not a virtue for red; it wants the world and wants it now.

Red is confidence. It is the color of life's unfolding drama, relating to our abilities to complete projects and attend to basic needs. Physicality is a hallmark of red, with strength of character as guide. As the red badge of courage, it is the color of bravery and heart. Red is the color of blood, the ties that bind, integrity, and family. Kin is "of the blood," joined together by the commonality of bloodline. Red, after the war is blessedly over, unites.

PINK The daughter of the morning star, pink is the symbol of all things feminine. Pink is as pink does, wondrously, wonderfully, and full of life-affirming energy. Pink is petals and powder puffs, ruffles, and frills. It is the epitome of health and forever young.

Pink derives its energy from red, yet is tempered and stilled. From this quietude, pink beckons as young lovers do. Calling out to us across spring-dappled days, with all the promise of a world in new bloom, pink regales the senses with softness. It gently nudges the child within to dreamy sleep. Rest assured, little one, pink loves and is love.

Quicksilver and light, pink comes on cat's paws to increase mental agility and expertise. Unnecessary detail is left in the wake of the color's demand for excellence. Students of life of all types are motivated by the color's restless wanderings. Pink intertwines playfulness with knowledge. Its young-at-heart sensibility doesn't allow for all work. Pink rambles and gambols, running away with emotion and scattering concepts in a haphazard way.

Pink loves people. Everywhere, every day, pink is the life of the party. Intense hot pink fills the body electric with charges of energy. It is derring-do and unpredictable, reveling in its own recklessness. Pink's plastic flamingos celebrate gaucherie on the lawn. It's a Las Vegas wedding chapel dressed up in pink neon. It's flaming pink, the oxymoron.

opposite: Red and orange highlighted with yellow suggest casual heat and invite the viewer to warm themselves deep in downy luxury.

right: Fantasy is the key, with red providing the ground.

Pink is the nonconformist in us. It revitalizes and reenergizes our nascent creative forces and blurs the distinction between our beloved fantasy and the lurking of evening-news reality. Create, begin, and begin again. Pink whispers that changes are afoot.

Pink is the Alice all little girls want to be, the white knee-socked, White Rabbit chaser of sunny childhood, full of curiosity and perky cute. We all want to experience Wonderland; we all want to go through the Looking Glass. Pink is there for us, to show us our younger selves, when life was long and days were short, when we disappeared down the rabbit hole as children and came out older, but perhaps not wiser, adults.

THE RULE OF 60-30-10

Breaking a room out into color elements is as easy as 60-30-10. The space you are to decorate with color will have separate percentages of differing hues. The largest expanses will be wall color, which represents approximately 60 percent of the color in the room. The second largest area of color will probably be window treatments, floor covering or upholstery; this is 30 percent. The 10 percent will be your accent color, which can be represented by floral arrangements, books, lamps, or other accent pieces.

Think of the space you are to decorate as clothing. When a man is formally dressed in a suit, the colors are broken out as follows: 60 percent of the color is the suit itself, the jacket and slacks; 30 percent is represented by the color of the shirt; and 10 percent is the color of the tie. Dress your rooms with colors broken down into 60-30-10, and you have a quick and easy color scheme.

above: In this Chinese nocturne, pink as lighting inspires a sense of wonder while appealing to our whimsical natures.

opposite: Red and pink tiles and a splash of tasty green set the table for a refreshing tropical delight. Casual dining is the order of the day as lively shades replicate the intensity of the color of the fruit.

YELLOW ORANGE
D YELLOW ORANGE GOLD YELLOW ORANGE
ORANGE

YELLOW /GOLD /ORANGE

YELLOW A DAY AT THE BEACH, YELLOW IS THE TAXI THAT CAN TAKE YOU AWAY

AND HOT BUTTERED POPCORN THAT MAKES YOU MELT AT THE MOVIES. AS

SUNLIGHT, IT THROWS THE LIGHT OF THE NEW DAY ON A NONSENSICAL WORLD,

BANISHING THE NIGHT AND CHAOS. THE WARMTH OF THE SUN TURNED TANGI-

BLE, YELLOW BECOMES FIELDS OF WHEAT, BECOMES MANNA RAINED DOWN

FROM HEAVEN. YELLOW SUSTAINS US AND ENTERTAINS US; IT'S OUR DAILY

BREAD AND CIRCUSES.

INNOCENT TRUST IS YELLOW. LACKING SUBTERFUGE, IT'S ALL RIGHT

THERE, IN PLAIN VIEW, FOR WHO CAN HIDE IN THE LIGHT OF DAY? CAT'S-EYE

CLEAR, YELLOW UNCOVERS THE TRUTH, SKETCHING HONESTY WITH SULFURIC

ACCURACY. YELLOW EXPOSES THE CYNIC TO BE JUST THAT.

above: Oranges tantalize while disappearing into a similarly valued orange wall. Edge
definition, which moves the object away from the wall, is provided by the lighter orange
color of the skin standing boldly against the pure white tabletop.

following page: Masculine-themed combinations are done up in casual colorations. Tweed
smoking jackets with leather patches at the elbows are the dress of the day as you read
Rudyard Kipling and talk seriously about little tin gods on wheels.

Yellow loves learning but can't sit still for long. Diverse concepts run haphazardly into one another to form, at first glance, strange bedfellows. But from these encounters come opposites that ultimately attract. The Odd Couple of colors, it's Felix-and-Oscar yellow.

Yellow is the symbol of the divine. Since time immemorial it has been associated with the sun. In Egypt, the sun god Ra ruled, the benign watcher in the sky. For the Greeks, Apollo's chariot blazed across the firmament, overseeing a Golden Age. Fra Angelico's saints were crowned with halos of yellow. It's Assisi's Brother Sun and Sister Moon. On the first day, God created yellow so we wouldn't go bump in the night.

Intense, flower-pedal-to-the-metal yellow is the color of strength and speed. From sports cars to sports heroes, all are adorned in lightninglike intensities of the color to denote inner power and determination. Flashy and hot, neon yellow lights up the night with blinking on-off enticements. The naked city is bathed in yellow after sundown, its irresistible siren's song beating a pulse in rhythmic yellow light that says, "See me." Yellow is the day, but today, yellow is also the night.

above: The yellow cabinet suggests intellect and high skill in combination with the cold seriousness of workaday gray steel handles.

opposite: Suggesting the warmth of the sun spun into fabric, these rugs simultaneously recall sunset in bright orange-red and the heat of the day in high-noon yellow.

GOLD All that glisters is indeed gold. That rarest of rare metals, gold, the alchemist's dream, has the power to change lives in ways alchemists could never achieve. It's the color of the sun, found deep within the bowels of the earth. People have lived and died for it, stolen and lied for it. There's gold in them thar hills, and the gold rush is on.

Greedy Midas has always beguiled us. It's the lure of the lira, the yen for the yen. Everyone wants

to be Rumpelstiltskin, spinning gold out of straw. Treasure chests full of gold doubloons sent men to watery graves. Great Train robbers and midnight grave robbers all lusted for the same thing. But remember the fate of Midas, unable to eat, the touch turned curse. When all is for gold, all is for naught.

From golden calves signifying ignorance and avarice to golden chalices that embody the Cup of Life, gold and spirituality have long been linked. Gold signifies the best we have to offer and that which we would give up gladly for our faith. Conversely, false gods are disguised for mass consumption in fake gold. It's fool's gold, the stuff of untruth.

Bands of gold are the ties that bind. There is much meaning in the simple and pure gold wedding ring. With this ring I thee wed, I thee pledge. Our greatest desire is to love and be loved, all wrapped around a little finger. Gold is undying love. It's promises fulfilled and wedding parties, golden memories, and golden anniversaries on hand.

Golden sunlight defines our days. It's the golden good morning of cakes on the griddle and golden slumbers when we lay down our heads. It's the Tupelo sweetness of the labor of bees, here in the land of milk and golden honey. It's golden delicious, keeping doctors at bay. Golden retrievers can be your best friend. Precious goldenrods flower in the sun-strewn summer fields of your fondest memories. It's the Golden Rule. Gold is the standard we set ourselves against.

ORANGE An everlasting revelation, orange is an every-evening, every-morning affirmation. Orange blazes in the sun's daily demise and phoenixlike rising, bathing the earth in gloriously toned light and

BOLD COLORS IN SMALL SPACES

Use bolder colors in small amounts or as overall coloration in small spaces to create a greater sense of excitement. These colors highlight items such as throw pillows on upholstery, lampshades, and various other accent pieces or give greater meaning to smaller spaces that don't have as much architectural interest, as in the case of spare bedrooms or baths.

PERSONAL STYLE

Your personal style is what really matters when it comes to color choice. This may not necessarily be fashionable, but if you are true to yourself, your rooms will shine with your colors. People will respond to these colors because they are representative of you and your family and your specific desires and emotions. Forget about fashion! The primary driving factor in interior design is personal style.

reminding us that tomorrow is coming, that tomorrows are always right around the orange corner and, hence, forgiving. Orange absolves yesterday's sins.

We are all made of clay. We are on and of the earth, we're all clay people. From *Angela's Ashes*, dust to dust, the orange men and women march through their terra-cotta times, often on clay feet. We light the way with science, knowing full well that this is all, that we are merely clay and no more. Clay is downright depressing.

As subtle as a hand grenade, orange crushes. In your face and up in arms, the color serves as call to action and call to caution. Bright warning signal of danger, the hue buries itself in the quick conscious, out of the corner-of-the-eye immediacy of escape and avoidance. Pay attention and save yourself; I am orange, proceed with care.

Orange signifies thoughtfulness and sincerity. Orange is selfless, recalling the bounty of the harvest and the season of sharing and celebration. The color of feasting and plenty, it symbolizes the fruits of summer's toil, full stores to last a full winter. We all partake in the feast and, at tables blessed with orange horns of plenty, give prayers of thanks.

Agent orange is provocateur. It is death and dying, fear and loathing in October. Vital green leaves turn orange in beautiful, final fury, raging against the dying of the light. Halloween symbolizes all souls in pumpkin orange jack-o'-lanterns with hollowed, hallowed triangular eyes and jagged, gap-toothed grins. Orange finds our own mortality, and we laugh, we trick or treat. It's a joke we all know; the end is the beginning. The infernal is infuriated and exits in embarrassed embers to orange peals of our laughter.

left: The color of the blanket relates to an overall sense of happiness and carries a feeling of summer in conjunction with the sky blue of the thread.

opposite: Terrene shades of
orange with mustard yellow
suggest a low-key approach to
dining. The primitive nature of
the two earthen elements is
given greater formality by the
white rims.

BLUE TURQUOISE

ISE BLUE PURPLE TURQUOISE BLUE PURPLE

TURQUOISE

BLUE/PURPLE/TURQUOISE

BLUE THE COLOR OF THE ETERNAL SKY, BLUE IS ALSO THE ALTERNATELY

SERENE OR WHIRLING WATER, TWO ELEMENTS THAT AFFECT OUR VERY LIFE

FORCE. FOR ANCIENT MARINER AND MODERN MIDSHIPMAN, THE DEEP BLUE

SEA IS HOME. RHYME AND CHANTY REGALE THE LISTENER, TELLING OF FLYING

DUTCHMEN AND DISASTERS OF TITANIC PROPORTIONS. THIS BLUE OF THE SEA

IS IN US AS WATER; WE ARE PART AND PARCEL OF THE DEPTHS. WE ARE MERE

SUBJECTS TO THE VAGARIES OF WIND AND WATER, BOBBING UPON THE SUR-

FACE, DANCING ACROSS THE WATERLINE. BLUE BUOYS US.

BLUE JAYS BATTLE BLUEBOTTLES; PERIWINKLE BENDS, SOFTLY

CARESSED BY BREATHS OF FRESH AIR. THE HEAVENS HOLD THROUGH SEVEN

INNINGS FOR THE BOYS OF SUMMER BEFORE THE ROLLING OF BLUE THUNDER. IN

WINTER'S HARSH REALITY, BLUE IS THE COLDEST OF DAYS, EARTH'S WARMTH

VANISHING IN THE CLEAR. WE TURN OUR FACES UPWARD AND SEE TOWERING

IMAGINARY CRITTERS, HORSES AND DOGS AND COWS, IN THE MARCHING MARSH-

MALLOW PUFF CLOUDS. OR WAS THAT JUST THE WIND? WE'RE ALL SKY PILOTS.

above: Playfulness and inner knowing are combined with beige, lying lazily against violet. The two rest assured on the mauve ground of the sofa, while relating to contrasting aspects or our personalities and healing our spiritual hurt.

following page: It's a spring fling done up in analogous lilac and cornflower blue. Gather 'round the maypole and let your cares drift into the gentle breeze. Dream your dreams with lavender linens and be young again, if only for a minute.

Everyone gets the blues, that melancholy of troubled waters that won't be stilled. Blue is unrequited love, the loss of a friend or the loss of our way. It is sorrow to the marrow. Yet somehow people find joy and happiness even in this. We sing the blues, raw and passionate, soaring in sadness or in smoky slow weeping wails. Through this music we give voice to the blues of life, and thus color our worlds in ways other than sight.

From the restful shades of indigo to the clarity of bright primary, blue creates stability and solidity. In its deeper values, blue can act as a grounding force in our lives. It's "true blue," steadfast and durable, compassionate and caring. Blue is emotion, as opposed to intellect. The blue tears of a clown are expressed by Verdi's *Rigoletto* and Chaplin's celluloid tramp. Blue is robin's eggs and Prussian kings, blue-eyed and innocent or a notorious bluebeard. It is ceruleans and cobalts, sapphires and topaz. The Blue Nile gave us watered-down civilization. Gainesborough's *The Blue Boy* and Picasso's Blue Period are art for our sake. The whole world is the big blue marble, and everything's gone ka-blue-ey.

PURPLE Arrogant and aloof, purple's kingship is a magical mystery, ages-old with secret knowledge covetously kept. The color of sorcerers and soothsayers, it is alive with symbolism, moving with the tide of time through eras of leaders born of the purple, from Augustus to Arthur, from Cheops to Charlemagne. Visionary purple is the power to lead.

Purple is the height of intelligence. All forms of thought, from the most arcane to the endless search for the philosopher's stone, are found in the hue. Purple is *The Thinker*, head resting on hand,

opposite: The blue of the hallway pulls us toward the white light. We move down the passage as souls drawn to the life force emanating at the end of the hall.

top: Decorate with sky blue, white, and turquoise to carve out a relaxing sanctuary. Pale blues are perfect for relaxation and contemplation, and best when accented with the warmth of wood for a touch of energy.

bottom: Blue, with its natural connection to water, promotes a sense of inner tranquility and calm. Enhance the soothing effects of a soak in a hot bath by decorating your bath with watery shades of blue glass tile.

dreaming up new answers to questions we have yet to ask. It is Galen's medicine, lasting for millennia, and the sudden stumbling onto petri-dish penicillin. Aristotelian and wizened or Newtonian and new, it expresses creativity, as in Michelangelo's Sistine Chapel or in the clockwork precision of Einstein's theory of relativity. Purple is the Muse.

Purple knows despair and grief, yet brings us the victory inherent in defeat. It is indefatigable, "The Charge of the Light Brigade" in full-galloping, death-rattling suicide. It is once more unto the breach, dear friends. It is once more unto Omaha Beach, dear friends. It is Nelson dying while triumphant at Trafalgar, but it is also Picasso's guilty *Guernica*, all anguish and hooves. It is Goya's *The Third of May 1808*, lined up against the wall. Defeat can mean victory and victory tastes of defeat, the sword of Damocles hanging by a single thread over purple's crown of thorns.

PROVEN COLORS

Take a close look at the colors you like to wear. These will help you to determine what colors to dress your interiors in. Do you like formal outfits with high contrast in black and white? Or do you prefer casual attire in flatter shades of green and beige? Check out what clothing you own before you shop for higher-end furnishings. Professional fabric buyers do this, first analyzing what is on the racks at department stores and then studying what is selling the most. That's why runway couture eventually makes its way into the home. After a color has proven popular as clothing, it is moved up into the higher price points of upholstery, window treatments and other "big ticket" home fashion items.

TURQUOISE Cheerful turquoise is the life of the color wheel. All giggles and silly smiles, its deeper self is hidden behind physical fun. The innate joy of the endless summer is tinted turquoise. Its *Beach Blanket Bingo* mentality relieves the fear of tomorrow, forever Annette, forever puppy love. Teenaged dreams are ringed in turquoise, splashing in waves of the wonder of it all.

Turquoise is the pristine of *Paradise Lost* and found, the desire for escape from society, the back-to-the-island draw. Under palm canopies and monkey laughter, the living is easy, and clothes not required. The Sargasso Sea separates us from our puritanical selves; we've gone native and like it. Wide-eyed and friendly, surreal Gauguin beasts surround us as we sip ice-cold color under tiny parasols, turquoise between our toes. Paradise never tasted so good.

Turquoise leads us to the tropical Never Never Land, where we are all Peter and Wendy, battling Hook and his pirates with logical laughter and illogical flight. We will never grow old, at least we don't believe we will, attached to barely visible blue-green strings as we fly across the stages of our lives. Clap your hands; Tinkerbell turquoise lives!

left: Days of old can be fantasy-filled. By marrying the sinuous white bureau with the solid, dark-valued wrought-iron chair, a contrast of emotion is created through opposites.

opposite: Contrasting values separate the pillow from the upholstery arm. The two are combined through the nature of the patterns.

GREEN
GREEN GREEN GREEN GREEN GREEN GREENGREEN
GREEN

GREEN

GREEN GLORIOUS GREEN PLAYS HIDE AND SEEK WITH THE SUN, WHICH PEEKS

THROUGH LEAVES OF GREEN WHILE YOU PONDER *LEAVES OF GRASS*. GREEN

IS THE KING OF IRELAND'S SON, NEW, FRESH, VITAL, AND A LITTLE LAZY.

SPROUTED FROM SEEDS, THE MIRACLE OF LIFE STUNS US EVERY APRIL. GREEN

IS THE VERDANT REMINDER THAT LIFE SPRINGS ETERNAL, FOR EVERGREENS

NEVER DIE.

FORESTS ARE DEEP IN GREEN MEANING. THE COLOR OF PHOTOSYN-

THESIS, GREEN TURNS LIGHT INTO LIFE. IT IS THE SYMBOL OF ALL THINGS

LIVING. GREEN SAPLINGS BEND IN THE WINDS OF CHANGE, YOUNG AND

STRONG, AND IN THEIR GREENNESS IS THEIR STRENGTH. FOR GREEN IS NEW,

NAIVE; GREEN DOESN'T KNOW THE DANGER. IT STANDS UP TO LIFE BECAUSE IT

CAN. TREMBLING ON TWO LEGS, GREEN SAYS I AM.

above: A sage green wall enhances the kitchen area, giving it over to the sense of taste. Eat your vegetables—they're good for you!

following page: Mata Hari would have loved this one. "Come into my parlor," said the spider to the fly. The seductress red will loverly you into telling all of your deepest secrets. But who cares? Damn the torpedoes, full speed ahead; tomorrow don't matter; I'm with the lady in red.

ACCENTING THE COLOR

In order to make colors flow through your home, take the overall color of one space and replicate it in seat cushions, matting on framed art, or as throw pillows in another space. Move colors about the home in this manner and the trip through the house will become more unified, as the thematic color is dispersed in other media.

Healing green mends broken bodies and minds. The medicine man rubs green herbs on the wounded knee; we lie down in green bowers to rest our weary heads. Cool green, served up as ointment to our troubled thoughts, eases the pain. It's the balm of the senses, *The Miracle Worker* green. Donning dark glasses, it soothes the sight. It's aromatherapy, the scent of fresh cut flowers. It tastes of the valley and feels like the sun. Green is the sound of hissing summer lawns. Green is the Band-Aid of the heart.

Quick-witted green flies Oscar wildly into the face of convention. Green is the comedian, the lithe leprechaun dancing around flames of words, talking nonsense. The color hides in riddles and hoards pot-o'-gold answers. The court jester in peat moss, green leaves you laughing. It's the homunculus, the little man leaping inside every cell.

Green sets the table for a feast of the senses. Farm-stand fresh and full of greengrocer goodness, green pleases the palate as well as the

opposite: Complements bring a feeling of royalty and tradition in the green field edged with deep pink.

top: Perfect in its bud as in its bloom, the sprouts arise to greet the day.

middle: Note how the hard surfaced vase is softened with pastel coloration and remains still, while the green represents motion.

bottom: The fragility of the white flower, tinged in green, is found in the softly drooping petals. The surrounding, nurturing green of the background is restful to the eye.

TINT YOUR CEILING

There is no law that says your ceilings must be white. When painting your room, add a dash of wall color to the ceiling white to tint it several shades up from your wall color. Try a tint of the wall color's complement (for example, a yellow ceiling with blue walls) to increase visual movement and vitality in the space. This same law applies to trim color; use the complementary hue of the wall color as trim to enliven a color scheme.

palette. Lettuce entertains you, and jalapeños leave you breathless. Green onions bring a tear to the eye. The guacamole is great; take a dip, try a bite. Oregano, you know, will spice up your life. Sage is for sages, and key lime is for pie. Spinach is tasty served straight from the can. Its save-the-day power makes Popeye de man. And when lunch is done, take a last sip of green tea, pay the bill with greenbacks, wipe your chin with green sleeves. Give the waitress a tip-of-the-iceberg lettuce and leave, green around the gills. It's a veggie delight—what a great way to say pass the broccoli, hold the relish. They're here again, salad days!

For green, the future is now. Soon the green of summer, the flowering of our lives, will turn to fall's dying dance. Green accepts the inevitability that all things must pass, yet it doesn't think about the end. It is F. Scott Fitzgerald and Zelda living life full in the zestful present tense with no past and nothing to come. It's carpe diem, seize the day. So let's drink and be merry, for tomorrow we may die. Green is the grasshopper whose future does not matter. Frankly, my dear, green doesn't give a damn.

opposite: Laughter and fun food are demonstrated in the green/red complements shown here. Green walls signify the space's nurturing aspects.

WHITE/GRAY/BEIGE/ BROWN/BLACK

WHITE THE TABULA RASA OF OUR LIVES, WHITE IS THE PLAIN WHITE SHEET WAITING TO HOLD OUR STORIES NOT YET WRITTEN. BASTIONS OF INNOCENCE COME CLAD IN WHITE. IT IS THE ANTITHESIS OF STREET SMARTS. WHITE BRINGS PEACE, WITH WHITE DOVES AND WHITE FLAGS OF SWEET SURRENDER. IT IS THE CLAPBOARD COLOR OF CHURCHES IN THEIR SUNDAY BEST. PURE AS THE DRIVEN SNOW, WHITE IS THE FAITH OF A CHILD; A BIT OF HEAVEN THAT'S LOST ITS WAY.

NEATNESS COUNTS FOR WHITE. CLEANSING, ANTISEPTIC WHITE ERADICATES GERMS. IT'S GENERAL HOSPITAL, ALL DONE UP IN WHITE LAB COATS AND CRÊPE-SOLED QUIET. AND, WHEN DOCTORS CAN'T CURE US, WHEN OUR RACE IS RUN, OUR SOULS FLY THROUGH THE WHITE CEILINGS AND PAST THE WHITE CLOUDS. OR WE STAY EARTHBOUND, THE GHOSTS IN THE ATTIC IN EPHEMERAL WHITE SHROUDS. DRIFTING WHITE IS OUR SPIRITS ESCAPING TRI-UMPHANTLY SKYWARD. WHITE IS OUR GOSSAMER WINGS. EVERYONE'S AN ANGEL IN WAITING.

above: Earthen and inviting colors are served up for casual dining in clay bowls with parchment beige cups. Stone is replicated in the cup form, and its rough-hewn aspects suggests the work of hands.

following page: The Black and Tan moves across the Irish hills to quell rebellion. Regimental black with beige and contrasting white tells of orderliness and purposefulness. The scene is softened by the nature of the striped cotton fabric and further related to the Guhrka through wicker. It's the Pax Brittanica; the bagpipes are singing; the Raj rules.

GRAY Dependable, durable gray is the whirring metal of well-oiled efficiency. It's the color of computers, the PC world in calculating gray.com. Gray is the industrial-strength color, served up in fifty-five gallon drums. It's the ten-penny nails that hold together the home. It's gray girders, the skeleton of the city. Gray supports our lives and does so without asking why, because Atlas never shrugged.

"There stands Jackson like a stone wall." Gray is the rock, and we call people we respect, who stand before enemy fire without flinching, names like Stonewall. Iron men, strong-willed men, sturdy and stern, are steely eyed, the Rocks of Gibraltar. And when they break the law, we send them to Alcatraz, the Rock, where they can break rocks. We're all in the Stone Age.

Gray is everyman. It's the man in the gray flannel suit, unobtrusive, just trying to fit in, one of the crowd. It's the lemmings that pour over the cliffs of life, never knowing, never caring, just gray and nameless. Yet gray is also the color of age, the length of days in salt and pepper hair, the seat of all wisdom. It is the good advice our fathers gave us, the recipe our mother's mother saved. It sways on porch swings and tells us tall tales. For gray will always love you, because you are the youth that gray was.

BEIGE Beige is the pliable, evanescent, molded plastic plywood of colors. Inspected and rejected, dejected beige is stuck in neutral. It is the Swiss government of the spectrum. Always reserved, forever the arbitrator, beige painstakingly does the background work, allowing the other colors to come out and play. It ubiquitously fits in, finds its place in line, disappears from conscious minds. It's that damned elusive Pimpernel, beige.

top: Comfortable brown surrounds the scene, while white banners gently formalize the space with vertical, free-flowing strips mounted at ceiling height.

bottom: Pristine and clear, these colors create specific object definition. The whiteness of the fruit is somewhat fantastic, as white is not what we would normally associate with real fruit.

opposite: The contrast of black with white is softened by the lazy, downward-moving nature of the sheepskin. The beige background unifies the two opposites.

HIGH VS. LOW CONTRAST

The high-contrast space is clearer and more highly defined than the low-contrast space. Use high contrast to enhance formality and low contrast to introduce soothing qualities. For example, black and white create a high contrast when paired, and this look is rather formal in feeling, while white with beige is softer and more casual.

Beige is the security blanket. It is the same-ness of the Sahara, the motionless Mojave, forcing us to believe in mirages of our own making. It's the sandman of silently shifting dunes and the long, slow caravan, numbing the senses in single-file dromedary drowsiness. Beige is the freight train that never ends, lulling us into cattle car–counting haziness while we wait, falling asleep at the wheel. It is the color of hypnosis: Your eyes are getting heavy, says the color. Fall asleep with me.

Beige is the color of disremembering, the color of missed appointments and people left standing. Tantamount to nothing, beige can't find its keys. Yesterday fades to beige in our memories. The hue of the twilight zone, the color of that period between sleep and wakefulness, beige is ultimately a gray area.

BROWN Brown is the cozy color, comfortable as the well-worn shoe, familiar as the old overcoat that never lets you down. Brown is the homburg hat of life. It is the furtive sip from the little brown jug that provides momentary warmth on cold winter afternoons. Good ol' Charlie Brown, ever sincere, always tries to kick the football, no matter how many times you pull it away.

Sticks and stones may break your bones, but brown will never hurt you. Brown is the Earth Mother. We all spring from the bosom of the soil. We are mud men and proud of it. Digging in the dirt, rooting around, we attempt to get at our

top: Rounded contours in beige give soft clues to our sense of touch. The calmness of the color relates to ease, with a slight bit of formality in the upright nature of white.

bottom: High summer is dressed down in light values of beige with white. A casual blonde tray suggests carefree mornings and starting the day off right with breakfast served up on an innocent white plate.

deepest feelings. The potting soil of the back porch of our minds gets under our skin as well as our fingernails. Brown is the color of inflection, reflecting nothing, keeping it all inside. It's the brown paper bag we put our souls in, letting them out at lunch.

Brown is the physical as opposed to the mental. Brown doesn't think too much, and when it does, it decides to go down with the ship. It will dance with who brung it. It is nonverbal, serving as a silent totem to our tribes. Brown is finally the forest we can't see through the trees.

BLACK Starless and Bible black is the color of the void. Forever night, the end of days is our greatest fear, expressed by black, the loaming in the gloaming, the gravedigger's friend. Black Death is coming, tall-hooded, to our horror. Murders of crows fluster, and witches take flight. When black is the color, none is the number.

Tradition is fringed in black. It has become the color of the past, the grainey Kodak past in which favorite aunts in '40s hairdos are young again, all forged in beautiful noncolor for us to find in basement drawers, dusty and saved, for whose posterity, we don't know. But there it is, our immediate sense of self, waiting for you to say, don't I look like them. They were me before me.

Fred Astaire wouldn't be the same without black. Done up in top hat and tails, special occasions are black's night out. Its formal, you-tango-divinely sensitivity is a natural for puttin' on the Ritz. Everyone feels more important in black. Men are more sophisticated, women more seductive. We're all Omar Sharif and Audrey Hepburn, and together we're stars. Black, the color of weekend millionaires.

Black is the hush-hush hue of the don't-tell secret. Blackguards plot in back alleys, and all bad guys wear black hats. Pencil-thin black moustaches are not to be trusted. Black is the color of the unknown, the black book, the Black Hand. Black keeps confidences, the private code of the soul.

top: The lighter-toned baskets are held down by the blue floor; otherwise they would seem to drift away into the light values of the wall.

bottom: Comfortable and nonverbal brown combines with clear, black-and-white checked pillows, which recall preciseness and cleanliness.

SECTION TWO

COLOR
FUNCTIONS

SERENITY CALM NURTURING TRANQUILITY SPIRITUALITY HEALING

COLORS FOR SERENITY

SERENITY SERENITY SERENITY SERENITY SERENITY SERENITY SERENITY SERENITY

SERENITY IS ESSENTIAL IN THESE RUSH-HERE, RUSH-HOUR-THERE LIVES OF OURS.

WE ALL SEARCH FOR PEACE IN OUR TIME, WHICH SOMETIMES SEEMS IMPOSSIBLE

IN A DYNAMIC AND CONSTANTLY CHANGING WORLD. TO INCREASE OUR SENSE OF

THE SERENE, WE CREATE PLACES OF CONTEMPLATION WITHIN THE HOME. IN ORDER

TO DESIGN A SERENE, RELAXING ENVIRONMENT WITH COLOR, IT IS NECESSARY TO

LOOK AT ALL THE ELEMENTS THAT GO INTO A ROOM. BY CHOOSING THE PROPER

COLOR PALETTE, YOU CAN DESIGN AN ENVIRONMENT IN WHICH TO RELAX AND

REFLECT—THE HOME AS REFUGE, AS THE SAYING GOES. MEDITATE ON THAT!

opposite: Orange walls delineated with white trim provide this bathroom with the feeling of sunset. The orange glow of the sun is translated into wall color relating to the end of day and a time for recovery, peaceful and alone with one's thoughts.

top: Overall blue is meditative. The room has Far East overtones as defined by the shape of the standing lamp, reminiscent of Oriental lanterns.

bottom: Cold, intense blue and hard, clear porcelain white define the space as active and serene. The white gives solid edge definition while the blue disappears at ceiling height, encapsulating the scene. The hard surfaces are softened by the blue tone's calming qualities.

opposite: Lilac is intuitive. Combined with blue and a hint of turquoise in the bed pillows, the room is almost clairvoyant in effect.

Analogous colors, colors located next to each other on the color wheel, produce serenity. To create an ambiance of tranquil understanding, combine turquoise with analogue blue, which provides aspects of truth and stability to the eternal nature of turquoise, representing clarity of thought. Medium red with orange yields an environment long on inner power with a foundation of earthiness. Try a combination of neutral tones, such as beiges with chocolate browns, to convey brown's feeling of comfort with the blending capabilities of beige. Deep or medium grays bring a sense of solid stone. Use with silent black and heavenly white to produce inner strength. Add a single bright red rose to the room to focus your moments of meditation.

Look to colors that have calming qualities in their darker values, such as blue, green, purple, brown, or gray for the dominant hue in the serene space. Accents can bring any number of secondary emotions to the room; choose red to signify the heart, medium intensities of pink for a sense of innocence, violet for friendship, or gold for permanence.

To accentuate the sacred aspects of a space, use dark purple with gold, which brings quietude with the dark value of purple while providing a feeling of the eternal with rich gold as the secondary hue. A third color can also be used to enhance the space. Green plants placed about

BRING THE OUTSIDE IN

Any interior environment is an attempt to replicate the outside world. Decorate your rooms in terms of color value just as the exterior environment is arranged, with darker values below (the earth), medium values as you move upward in a space (trees, hills, and mountains), and lighter values at ceiling height (sky). It's your world, and welcome to it!

left: This is a welcoming sight after a hard day at work. Serenity as a form of escape is found here. Browns and beiges combine to reduce stress through analogous combinations.

the room, as the healer, or black accents, such as wrought iron, impart a sense of the past. While away the hours on a trip through time with royalty and luxury calming the senses.

Similarly toned colors in dark, middle, or light ranges also effect a calming interior. Blue married with terra-cotta shades of orange is grounding, representative of the totality of earth and sky. Winter whites with light blues create a silent winterscape. Green with analogous yellow is relaxing and summery, while deeper shades of orange with brown give a sense of long evenings surrounded by silent fall colors.

When medium to dark orange is used as the largest color in a space, its sublime power and representation of the earth will produce a serene effect. Partner this with verdant, medium greens and bark browns as counterpoints to give the room a calm coolness that recalls the restfulness of a stand of trees at sunset. To complete the scene, use faded beige as an accent color in decorative objects that have a tumbled-stone quality, bringing the outdoors in and creating your own indoor garden getaway.

Green always helps promote relaxation. Dark green walls add a forestlike quietude and seclusion to a room. Use a medium beige color for the trim to define the edges of your arboretum. Add rough saddle-leather upholstery to suggest ruggedness, orange for casual comfort, or accents regal red to promote formality and family ties.

top: Mauve wall color is impacted by blue values lying "underneath" the color. The serene aspects of mauve are given further focus by the contradictory red table. Flora tells a natural tale in its upward-reaching appearance.

bottom: Heaven in a wild flower, eternity in an hour. This forever flower, imitating the forever sun, blooms blessed in the brazen colors of the day, orange and yellow. It thus sends sunshine back to the sun. It's infinity at your feet.

opposite: Serenity is achieved here through the use of alternating vertical stripes that enclose the environment with an overall sense of stability and protection, even though the coloration is lively. Deep values of pink are sedating.

Crimsons and burgundies are soothing in leathery coolness. As wall color, deep crimson imparts a sense of inner calm. Utilize blue as a secondary color and the room becomes restful, with overtones of tradition and stability. Add a pair of brass lamps with black shades; the opaque shades provide a quiet lighting effect as they throw the yellow light of incandescent bulbs vertically, creating pools of light.

BLACK ACCENTS

Remember this perhaps apocryphal saying in interior design, "Every room should have at least one black piece in it." When you place a black object in a space, it creates the somewhat bizarre effect of enhancing the other colors in the room. Try it, it works!

left: Lilac walls and the cornflower blue bed covering and artwork give an atmosphere just right for lazy days lost in thought, especially when the space is infused with pink light created by the pleated shade. The purple hues of the wall color relate to mental activity, while the blue emphasizes peaceful coexistence.

opposite: Serene thoughts are communicated through the use of earthen shades of orange. Countered by the lightness of white sheers firmly attached to the wall with a wrought-iron rod, the room gives a feeling of calm tinged with restful escape from the exterior heat.

following page, left: Cool blue tranquilizes, medium values giving way to the lighter shade above. All is monochromatic quiet; you could hear a pin drop as your eye moves down the wall to the break in the color, signifying an open door to another space.

following page, right: Analogous color combinations— in this case teal walls with indigo upholstery—provide a restful place for the eyes. Define shape with complement orange to clarify objects floating in a green haze of dominant color.

Lighter shades of lilac with pink give a space an effervescent, uplifting feel, somewhat like an Oriental garden in spring—calm and tranquil. Contain the feeling of airiness by defining the space with the pure aspects of white as a trim color. Use hints of saffron yellow and mint green to increase the room's vitality and give a sense of the here and now. These combinations also are reminiscent of floating and a lightness of being, as well as the associations they bring of the higher self and intuition. When searching for serenity, look no further than home. For home is where the art is, and an artfully colored home can do wonders for the heart.

above: Relax in the serenity of simple colors. This space is serene due to the use of monochromism. The deep clay of the walls is replicated in the chair fabric.

opposite: Dressed down for comfort, clay as a large block of wall color defines the space . The color invites and pulls the viewer inward toward the casually done up white sofa. The wall color is carried into the scene via the large throw pillow on the left, which helps to unite the divergent values of light-toned beige and deep orange.

COLORS FOR FANTASY

FANTASY FANTASY FANTASY FANTASY FANTASY FANTASY FANTASY

ZFANTASY PLAYS AN IMPORTANT ROLE IN OUR LIVES. IT SPURS THE IMAGINATION IN

ESCAPES AT THE MOVIES AND FEEDS OUR SENSE OF WONDER DURING TRAVEL AND

DAY TRIPS TO THE MUSEUM. THE STIMULATING SPACE ENCOURAGES OUR INTEL-

LECT TO INTERACT WITH OUR EMOTIONAL SELVES, ALLOWING FOR THE FANTASTIC

IN OUR LIVES AND PLEASING THE ARTIST IN US ALL.

EACH COLOR ON THE COLOR WHEEL HAS ASSOCIATIONS WITH MENTAL

OR PHYSICAL ACTIVITY, OR IT IMPARTS RESTFUL QUALITIES THAT HELP TO BALANCE

THE ACTIVE NATURES OF THE OTHER COLORS. WHEN DEFINING THE FANTASY-FILLED

SPACE, THINK IN TERMS OF MOTION. WARM COLORS SUCH AS RED, YELLOW, AND

ORANGE HAVE OBVIOUSLY ENERVATING ASSOCIATIONS. BLUE, GREEN, AND PURPLE

ARE TRADITIONALLY SEEN AS SEDENTARY. USE COMPLEMENTARY COLOR SCHEMES

above: A fun-loving, pink fur rug on the floor sets the stage for dreamscapes full of fantasy. The upward-moving nature of white interplays with the earthy tones on the walls. Note the intense lavender chest to the right, which adds to the unreal quality of the space.

that incorporate both sides of the color wheel to establish the active nature of a room while also including the emotional elements you wish to highlight. For example, marry stable navy blue with humble medium values of orange to impart comforting qualities to a room. This creates a low-key environment that still imparts activity through complementary color use.

The active room usually relies on light values. Ban the night with yellow walls. Then, for a secondary color, choose your season: pastels for spring, or more intense values of green to keep the warm glow of summer all year long. Add natural cottons in whites and beiges as upholstery fabric or as slipcovers, which recall casual summer clothing, loose-fitting and lightweight.

Color can help point the way. It leads us down corridors and serves as a signpost. In this sense, color in interiors focuses the activity of the home. By decorating our spaces with color for various activities, we furnish easy definitions for these spaces. The living area can be designated as highly formal with medium to light values. Increase the formality of a room by accenting with elements of precious metal, or tone things down with primitive pottery. Casual corners in family rooms can be

established with brown leather chairs for intimate late-night chats. Kitchens, essentially workplaces, can be delineated with bright values that ease the workload and help the imaginative chef stir up some creativity.

Primary colors stimulate learning. Reds, blues, and yellows impart solid, attention-getting edge definition for the kids. This helps them to define shapes and learn about their environments. For teenagers, memory gets a nudge from red. Intellectual yellow impacts our logical selves and aids in cognition, helping with homework. Verbal skills are heightened with light values of talkative green. Decide which skills you would like to enhance in your child, and then choose colors that address these areas.

above: Intensity and strong feeling are incarnated in this red-rimmed fantasy. Translucent white glass calls attention to the shape of the lamp. The picture leaning against the wall is bordered in white, giving space definition through contrast with the deep pink at the center.

opposite: Red and pink endow this space with heat. Pink adjusts the temperature a little more to the cool side. Further turning down the thermometer is the blue cushion on the right, while the beige cushion on the left goes with the flow and leaves pink to tell its tale.

following page, left: Contrasting values as well as the overall coloration can impact a space, causing objects to recede or move outward toward the viewer. Note how the red flower disappears into the similarly colored wall while simultaneously leaping out from the pink wall.

following page, right: Enveloped in the fantastic, pink surprises as a translator of the solid form of the table leg. Alternately, it subdues with the soft texture of the ground fabric, long and luxurious.

above: In "Death of a Wrestler" by René Magritte, the rose consumes the room. Here, the red rose consumes the eye, exploding ever toward the viewer and stimulating both the kinesthetic and olfactory senses.

right: Surreal red moves mass and weight around, rearranging the scene. The overall sense of motion runs away from the viewer and creates a feeling of wonderment as inanimate objects turn lively.

following page, left: Sage green and poppy yellow dance effortlessly across the turquoise-flecked countertop, asking the viewer to move with them on their conga-line to the edge. Animated colors move through the scene, presenting a cartoonish quality of bright hues.

following page, right: Pink contrasts the stern aspects of the blue wall, giving the space a non-conformist feel. All of the staidness of the wall color goes for naught when confronted with the spring-like values, giving the geometric form of the upholstery a sprightly push over the edge of form.

Any time, place, or lifestyle can be replicated with color use. Determine who or what—or even when—you want to be, then go after the color that captures those feelings. Impart a sense of the past by choosing traditional colorations; more casual colors can take us to far-off postcard places. Overall colorations such as Wedgwood blue for walls with white trim reminds us of dainty upper-class eighteenth-century life. Re-create a tropical paradise using turquoise color schemes with white upholstery and clay-colored accents.

We can all live like kings, dressing our rooms in rich purple upholstery, or rule as Egyptian pharaohs with turquoise and gold accent pieces scattered about the home. Perhaps a Mexican fiesta is your cup of tea? Pull bright colors from serapes—intense reds, yellows, and greens—for sofa scarves and toss pillows, then combine with faux-painted walls in rustic whites and beiges. Serve up a waxed pine trunk with black wrought-iron clasps for your cocktail table, and mix in pine seventeenth-century Spanish-flavor chairs with

above: Pink married to red is particularly vulnerable in feeling. The strength of the deeper red value overwhelms the pink, creating a sense of movement and stimulation.

opposite: Too hot to touch, the red bed calls out, inviting passion plays full of burning sensuality. Bathed in red oneness, this scene allows for little else but thoughts of love and togetherness.

above: Fantastic flowers leap up from deep lilac to pervade our sense of wonder. Lively light green increases the whimsical nature, while white gives a sense of youthful innocence.

left: Stimulating hues can also function in spaces designated for rest and reflection. Decorating with high color contrast imparts an attraction of opposites, delightfully innocent in shades of spring. This entices the viewer with the eagerness of blonde wood floor together with purple bed covering and lilac artwork.

PULL COLORS FROM THE LARGEST PATTERN

Select the largest pattern in a space first, then pull your dominant room color from the pattern. Upholstery, an oriental rug, or a window treatment will generally contain the room's largest pattern. Artwork can also serve this purpose. This is much easier—and less expensive—than painting the walls first and then trying to find appropriate color matches on the marketplace in interior furnishings, as these will be subject to fashion dictates.

COLOR CHANGES COLOR

Pay special attention to colors incorporated together in the same room, as each color will be affected by its placement in relation to other colors. Colors will be impacted by surrounding colors, causing shifts in the tonality. For example, at times when using white with beige, the white can appear "dirty" due to its proximity to the darker value of beige.

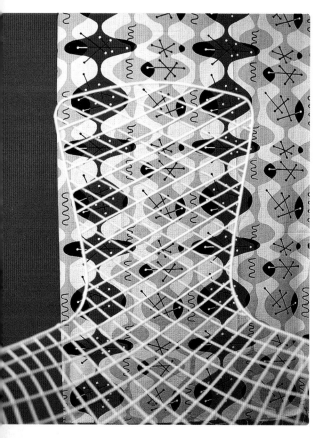

above: Hot complements playfully attract the viewer in contrast to the hard-to-grasp gray and white grounds. The wire chair in white is contoured with openness, suggesting a parabolic sense of motion.

opposite: Yellow walls happily regale the senses with memories of sunlit days and the naive sense of childhood.

rush seats for occasional seating. Accent with rough-textured baskets and primitive clay pottery to complete your south-of-the-border bolero.

Stimulating colors are often seen in electric intensities. As such, they are considered in conjunction with the contemporary in design. These colors are the children of the twentieth century, and they reflect the immediacy of the now. Use electric hues sparingly, as slip-seat fabric for dining chairs, lampshades, or as accent pillows on upholstery rather than as a dominant overall color. These colors best serve as a hot counterpoint to neutral interiors that incorporate beige, gray, white, and black rather than as large, overwhelming blocks of wall color.

From the shock of hot pink to the loudness of opera-singing orange, the fantasy-filled environment includes colors and color combinations that are, at times, unexpected. Flights of fancy take wing when we use color imaginatively. Cupid is inspired by red in romantic fantasies. Green can startle with freshness, and mild blue can turn bold. Dividing your space with active colorations lets you be the guide to the realm of the senses. Find your bliss, then color your world with it.

HEALING

EALING HEALING

HEALING HEALING HEALING HEALING

HEALING

COLORS FOR HEALING

COLOR HAS BEEN USED AS HEALER SINCE TIME IMMEMORIAL. WHEN TAKEN

IN LARGE DOSES OR SMALL, HEALING HUES ARE THE SHAMAN OF THE SENSES,

REENERGIZING THE WEARY AND CALMING THE ANXIOUS. WHEN INGESTED BY THE

VIEWER, THESE COLORS CAN PROMOTE A HEALTHIER, HAPPIER LIFE. SIMPLY

SURROUNDING YOURSELF WITH LIFE-AFFIRMING COLOR CHANGES YOUR THINK-

ING AND PROVIDES SOMETIMES SUBTLE, SOMETIMES DRAMATIC CHANGE.

HOWEVER IT IS USED, COLOR IS A TOOL FOR FIXING WHAT AILS US. THE DOCTOR IS

IN, IN A COAT OF MANY COLORS.

above: Healing red relates to the blood that flows through us all. Note how the darker values on the right in the upholstery fabric pull your attention to the right side of the frame first.

First among the healers of the color wheel is green. Green is nature's visual muscle relaxant. In dominant hue, either light valued or dark, green assuages. Use it in its dark ranges as a thematic color to calm, or in lighter values to revitalize. Marry green wall color to analogous blue upholstery to create a liquidity of motion and a semblance of ease. In combination with yellow, it serves up refreshing vistas, healing through the suggestion of the lazy days of summer and the newness of spring.

Red is the color of the blood that courses through our veins. In this sense, the color is reassuring and constant, reminding the viewer of healthy existence, and has been long held as a symbol of well-being. Red is the glow of the fire that fuels our imaginations and provides for meditative thought. We stare endlessly into red flames and feel calmed and warm. And, of course, red is love, and knowing that we are loved always makes the heart pump faster. The space defined by red speaks of sensuality and touch, massaging our cares with *amore*. Relax in a red

left: Red, white, and pink heal through the suggestion of purity represented by the white day-bed and the *joie de vivre* of pink.

opposite: A pervasive sense of health and well-being is conveyed by the womblike atmosphere shown here.

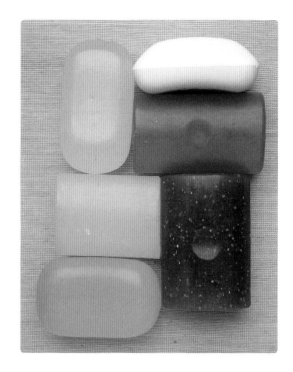

above: Green soap brings the healing power of green to clean. And cleanliness is next to godliness, which we would assume is a good thing. So wash up! Physician, heal thyself with green.

opposite: Communication of our inner worlds is represented by lilac with brilliant white, giving a heavenlike appearance to the space. Soul mates talk to one another, alone together.

leather chair to be reminded of tradition and the balm of brandy on a cold winter's night. Red combined with green tells of high holidays, of being surrounded by the healing power of family and dear friends.

White is the epitome of health. In representing cleanliness, it shortens the time we feel pain. White sheets beckon us to lie down and free ourselves from the hurt of movement and the aches of long days. White walls calm the senses through the very lack of distracting color. White distills the environment, washing the space in whiteness and removing harmful elements, and, in so doing, erasing our worries as well. When combined with blue walls, white upholstery is refreshing breaths of fresh air, cloudlike in feel. White linen tablecloths stimulate the sense of taste by removing potentially clashing colorations from the scene. Partner white with turquoise to suggest clear thinking and feelings of health.

TESTING YOUR COLORS

Be sure to take a look at fabric and paint swatches in the environment in which they will be placed. View the color at different times of day, paying close attention to the color during the time you are most in the space. For example, look at the swatch under artificial light at night, if that is primarily when you use the room.

Purple is associated with the mind and emotion. This color impacts our mental health, especially when incorporated with healing green. A space with light values of purple is mentally invigorating, clearing up the miasma caused by the very dynamism of life. When yellow serves as secondary color to purple, attentiveness elevates; with green, mental acuity is slowed. Purple is the emotional healer; it serves to penetrate to the source of psychic pain and bring curative power to those suffering from inner hurt.

top: Cool green cabinets serve as home to transparent blue water. This picture of health is accentuated by the white walls that frame the scene.

bottom: White suggests a healthy lack of distracting color. We all need a break from the perception of color, at times. White relieves the eye and gives us a shot at visual recovery.

opposite: Health-giving green with lilac relates to the slowing down of mental acuity, just in time for a quick siesta. The room is active in coloration, yet softer values are used to denote peace. Each color represents a different aspect of the space. Note the use of complementary color on the wall trim.

following page, left: Overall, black is healing, as in the placidity of the starry night.

following page, right: Summer clouds surround the chef. The airiness of the blue wall is enhanced by the whiteness of the cabinet.

Brown is often used on upholstery in casual scenarios such as family rooms—a welcome retreat after a hard day. Beige induces healthful sleep, providing respite in its unchallenging nature and curing with its restorative qualities. Incorporated with brown, the protective feeling of analogous closeness envelopes us in folds of comfort. Bedrooms casually dressed with the protective nature of brown for wall color as cuddle-up bed coverings hasten dreamy sleep. Color is the medicine we take when we're in need. So take your medicine; it's the color-doctor's orders.

FORMALITY VS. INFORMALITY

Complementary color schemes are more formal in feeling than analogous schemes, which tend to be more restful. Use complementary schemes (red/green or blue/yellow) in medium to light values in the formal areas of the home, such as the living room or dining room. Save analogous schemes for family rooms and bedrooms, where respite is desired.

top left: The saving grace of blue walls helps pull the viewer toward the green tabletop. Healing is conveyed through the green in combination with a slight glimpse of orange, which relates to calmness and repair.

above: Healing is found in unassuming beige. This bedroom lulls us to sleep with beige as unchallenging somnambulist.

opposite: Beige softens the contemporary line of the sofa, while the silvery gray pillow is used as a counter. Note the sense of primitive fantasy in the clay accent pieces on the mantel.

When your thoughts race and your heart pounds, blue soothes. The color acts as a grounding force in our lives, enhancing meditative skills. Blue is the sedative of the senses. Other more numinous attributes of the heavenly hue bring blue out of the realm of the purely physical and into the mystic of the metaphysical.

Blue expands our sensitivity to the needs of others and our ability to get in touch with our own feelings. The nonverbal cues that we pick up from blue include those of tradition and that of belonging to a group. Blue conveys this sense of safety within the confines of the group and thereby increases our sense of worth and value as contributors to society. We are the Blue Man Group.

above: Lavish lilac colors the walls, relating to our internal psyches, while beige sets the stage for the healing power of inner peace found in this room. Stable blue on the throw pillow with blonde wood tables continue the similarly valued story, increasing the lighter-than-air feeling of floating in space. Transcendental healing takes place in rooms such as this.

opposite: Dark values of blue call out to comfort us. We are drawn to the dark-valued bed, wanting to stretch out and close our eyes for just a few minutes. Note the comfortable chocolate brown, which adds to the serenity of the space.

CLARITY CLARITY

CLARITY CLARITY CLARITY CLARITY CLARITY

COLORS FOR CLARITY

USE COLOR TO HEIGHTEN CLEAR THINKING AND FURTHER YOUR INTELLECTUAL

PURSUITS. CLEARLY DEFINE EACH INDIVIDUAL ELEMENT IN THE ROOM, GIVING IT A

SPECIFIC PLACE OF ITS OWN, BY COMBINING DIFFERENT HUES WITH NEUTRALS

SUCH AS PURE WHITE OR BEIGE. THIS CREATES AN ENVIRONMENT THAT IS CON-

DUCIVE TO SKILL AND CRAFT, THE WORK OF OUR HANDS AND MINDS AND, THUS,

OUR HEARTS. GOD IS IN THE DETAILS, AND THE DETAILS ARE MULTIHUED.

ACHIEVE CLARITY WITH COMPLEMENTARY, AS OPPOSED TO ANALOGOUS,

SCHEMES. THESE COLORS, OPPOSITES ON THE COLOR WHEEL, ALWAYS CREATE A

DISTINCT DIVISION OF COLOR WHEN THEY ARE PAIRED. INCORPORATE VARYING

VALUES OF COMPLEMENTARY COLORS IN A ROOM TO HEIGHTEN PERCEPTION, AS

THE TONAL CONTRASTS ARE IMMEDIATELY NOTICEABLE.

opposite: Orange-finished kitchen cabinetry is clearly apart from the dining area, done up in black and white. Note how colors are moved from one space to another, thereby providing a unifying effect. Metallic silver is pulled from the wall splash in the kitchen into chairs and the table base.

Light tones on dark grounds are delineated from their surroundings. They send messages that there are functional differences between the shapes found in a room, such as a white mantel standing highly defined against a red wall. This sense of clarity is important to use as a definer of space, whether active or passive. Complementary color schemes are more formal in feeling, while the opposite is achieved when using analogous colors that fade into each other.

Black with white is the essence of opposites, providing a no-nonsense atmosphere. The absence or addition of light (which black and white represent) relieves the eye of the burden of color definition, freeing us to search out more lofty goals. Clinical in nature, white, when used in toned-down values as a wall color, eases eye strain, while black serves as counterpoint, clearly stating line. Large squares of black and white tile have long been identified as traditional flooring; zebra 'stripes add a dash of black/white animal sensitivity to any room. The formal black sofa

above: The white towel is obviously separated from the overall blue tone of the space.

opposite: Note how the darker floor, medium wall values, and lighter ceiling delineate each area of the space, as in the exterior environment: dark-valued earth, medium values as seen in trees, and lighter sky above.

leaps from the white-defined interior, while white faux fur on the floor is art deco chic. Black, white, and gray have also made the transition to contemporary styles in the products of the post modern; the kitchen with stainless steel appliances and black granite countertops surrounded by white cabinetry speaks volumes about serious cooks.

When looking for clarity, look particularly to spring, which is captured in colors that bring the season of renewal indoors. Use sprays of flowers, whether in natural bunches or formally arranged, to freshen your interiors. Light values are always springlike. Yellows, pinks, and lavenders create a visual impact and also remind us of the fresh scent of spring. To soften a room and make it more feminine and wistful, use saffron as a wall color, pink bed coverings, and white lace window treatments. Hotter intensities convey the vitality of the season and can dress up the lowly spare bedroom with shots of soft color.

Orange is a clarion call to the senses. Transcendent in nature, orange creativity is the warm glow of inner knowledge. Clearly cutting through the clutter, orange hops to attention and regales the senses. Cool down the orange-walled room with green for the upholstery or as a window

above: Clearly the plant is not part of the vase, though the stem color is replicated by the transparent green. Springlike in feel, the scene recalls the yellow of the sun, found in the tabletop; green symbolizes living things in the vase form; and pink is related to the season of renewal.

below: The shoji screen is protective yet semi-transparent; its white panels crossed by black lines represent orderliness. The scene is relieved by the patterns on the delft bowls and the natural form of the flowers.

opposite: The colors are playful and casual in this dining area, seeming to dance around the tabletop. Geometric forms—the rectilinear chairs, box-like server, the rigid line of the ceiling beam, and the compass curve of the doorway arch—are the order of the day, and each aspect is called out by an individual color.

COLORS WITHIN COLORS

All colors are affected by the surrounding colors. Look to the color beneath the color for direction. For example, mauve is a pink with blue undertones. So combining mauve with blue will pull the blue from the mauve to a greater degree than if you choose to downplay the color's blue base by using another color with no relation to blue, such as yellow.

above: Turquoise tile is slick and reflective, clearly defined by the white grout and the tub. The aquatic nature of turquoise increases the cool sensuality of the bath.

left: The mantel, done up in white, stands out starkly against the deep red wall. The white color gives the mantel solid edge definition, which adds to the sense of objectivity.

treatment. Use orange with white accents or trim color to impart a greater sense of clarity to the space. Orange focuses attention on itself at the expense of other objects, so when you incorporate it into your décor as an accent, sprinkle with care.

Red is for remembering. It is hard to forget the girl in the red dress or the red sports car that careens by outside your window. When memory needs help, red pinpoints the object and renders it

LOCAL COLOR

Many areas of the world are associated with specific colors and color combinations. Study up on the cultural implications of color use in your world, or choose colors associated with your particular locale. For example, blue with white and yellow many times references nautical motifs and is often seen in coastal locations, while turquoise is associated with the American Southwest.

above: Surrounding everything, white defines the beginning and ending of objects. This increases the sense of clarity and allows for ease of concentration.

opposite: Clear thoughts are focused by the bright images on the wall, which alternately pull the viewer in and move thoughts outward from the blue ground with orange border.

above: Decorate with sky blue, white, and turquoise to carve out a relaxing sanctuary. Pale blues are perfect for relaxation and contemplation, and best when accented with the warmth of orange for a touch of energy.

opposite: Differing shades of blue move the eye down and inward toward the flat surface and the barstools. The different values of blue help to identify areas and guide our motion towards the scene.

left: The wall is obviously delineated from the mantel by the clarity of red and white. The scene is unified, however, by pulling the red of the flames out as wall color, spreading the warmth throughout the room.

opposite: Large blocks of color clearly state purpose. This room is meant for reflection and clear thinking, a retreat in red designed for study centered around the warmth of the white fireplace.

easy to recall. A color that clearly separates itself from the pack, red highlights and is quick to draw attention. Choose red for upholstery to convey a sense of immediacy and sensuality. As floor covering, red delineates a space as special and regal. Red combined with blue relates to tradition, as in the Heriz Persian rug. In contemporary venues, red

picture frames call attention to the photos they hold. Create playful environments using bright red accents. A red-accented kitchen is purposeful with a side order of creativity. Clarity in color use is the key to rational, forward-moving thought processes because, as we all know, in a clear room you can see forever!

NURTURING
NURTURING
NURTURING NURTURING NURTURING

COLORS FOR NURTURING

NURTURING IS ALL ABOUT LOVE: LOVE OF OURSELVES AND OUR NEAREST AND

DEAREST. IN THIS LOVE WE SHOW CARING, WE COMFORT, WE TENDERLY SEE TO THE

NECESSARY ASPECTS OF LIVING. LIKEWISE, SUSTAINING OURSELVES IS OF PREEMI-

NENT IMPORTANCE, FOR WITHOUT IT WE OBVIOUSLY CAN'T GO ON. WE MUST CARE

FOR OUR PHYSICAL BODIES, FEEDING, PROVIDING WATER, CLEANSING, AND

RESTING. SEEING TO OUR EMOTIONAL WELL-BEING IS ALSO PARAMOUNT IN

ORDER TO LEAD A FULL LIFE. ENHANCE THESE PROCESSES BY USING COLOR'S

ASSOCIATIONS AND STIMULATIONS. HAVE YOU HUGGED YOUR INTERIOR DESIGN

TODAY? HAS YOUR INTERIOR DESIGN HUGGED YOU?

above: Nurture your cares away. Daily stresses need to be relieved. The inviting bath in hard white porcelain is softened by the deep pink above the wainscotted lower wall. Tender coloration relates to our inner child.

STAGES OF LIFE

Think about who will be using a room before you decide on color. Relate the colors you choose to the ages of the inhabitants. Soft pastels keep an infant's environment soothing, while primaries in their brazen brightness are often used to invigorate the older generations.

Nurturing others is a corollary of the maternal instinct and is a significant factor in our lives as social beings. Environments colored in dedication to our emotional selves activate certain feelings that we would like to encourage, while also elevating the nurturing sides of our personalities. Red relates to love, purple addresses inner peace, and blue represents security.

right: The color of the sky lassoed and brought to earth in wall color. This room belies any possible staleness with blue transferring the outdoors in. And, as fresh air tends to make one feel drowsy, the room creates its own!

COLOR AND ARCHITECTURE

If you live in a style of home that has historical reference, study the colors that are associated with that particular style. Medium to dark greens are popular in arts and crafts style; a particular shade of medium blue is associated with federal style while deep red is seen as an important element of Victoriana.

left: Red, seen here with a white border, relates to the appetite and is often used in restaurants to stimulate our desire for nourishment. The atmosphere is inviting and clearly defined for dining.

To impart a sense of nurturing to a space, turn to earthen colors, utilizing greens, oranges, and browns as thematic colors in a room. In their deep values, they act as protector and comforter, conveying a nonverbal sense of care. We surround ourselves with these colors and feel at peace. Use them to best advantage in areas of the home designated for retreat, security, and peace—family rooms, bedrooms, and studies—the places we seek out, intentionally or unintentionally, when we feel a need to recover. Dressing these rooms in colors representative of Mother Earth relates to care and nurturing in its elemental sense.

left: This green umbrella serves as stand-in for the sheltering green canopy of the forest.

below: Mother Nature to the rescue! The various browns of the floor and the vertical brown tone in the background combined with green walls suggest the nurturing aspects of the forest, a place of shelter from the storms of life. Take a close look at the photo. The longer you stare at it, the more quiet and forest-like it becomes.

opposite: Cool forest hues united with playful, physical turquoise define a dining area that is fun to eat in and good for you. The analogous nature of the two greens is brought into focus by the orange of the plant.

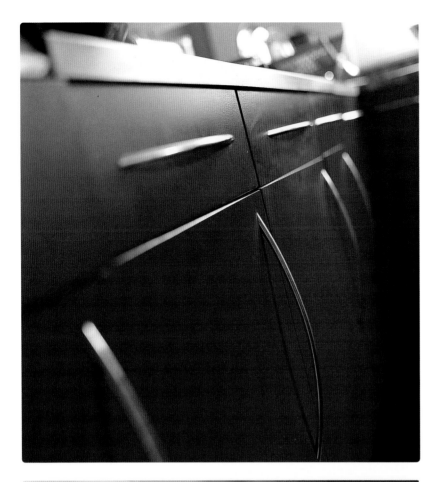

Colors have the ability to communicate complex emotions. Use them to speak of tenderness (try pink ranges for walls), sympathy (blue), and compassion (red). Bring blue in differing values into a space to connect with our caring natures and provide a space that is welcoming, offering a sense of understanding without saying a word. Reds come straight from the heart, getting to important issues with firm resolve and a desire to help. Yellows and greens promote activities that feed both the mind and the body. Green especially suggests health-giving vegetables, while yellow replicates sunshine and the energy it produces.

Color provides stimulating environments when the activity calls for it or, alternatively, slows down the senses at times when we require reenergizing. Use complementary schemes for activity and analogous schemes to reduce stress. Red has long been considered as stimulating to the appetite. But should you desire to suppress your appetite (and can't we all stand to lose a little weight?), give the dining area blue-toned walls, as blue is rarely found in nature as foodstuff. Bracing air to fill our lungs is suggested by employing lighter values of blue that recall the sky for the main thematic color

previous page, left: Represented in the stove front and the walls, analogous colors green and blue relate to the sky and the greenery of the earth, bringing the goodness of the outdoors in. Fresh and vital, the space tells us that nourishment is to be found within.

previous page, right: A sage green wall enhances the kitchen area, giving it over to the sense of taste. Eat your vegetables; they're good for you!

top: Red cabinets signify that something special lies inside. Soothing, hard stability in red married to gray steel handles relate to ease of access and the clean tools of the chef, stainless and sharp-edged.

bottom: Hard-surfaced red holds food for thought. This refrigerator, done up in fire-engine red, demands to be opened, sharing the goodness within.

opposite: Orange and white provide a nurturing appeal, combining the elemental nature of the sunset with the white surface of spiritual communion.

above: Blue in both medium and dark values accentuates the orange of the earthy goodness of the harvest. This creates a bountiful atmosphere, serene and right on time for dinner. The totality of the exterior world is suggested in the blueness of sky, combined with the goodness of the earth represented in the orange hue.

below: Orange with blue signifies a juicy delight served up in complementary fashion. The deepness of the wall tone highlights the ripeness of the fruit, making the viewer want to reach out and take a bite.

opposite: Blue food is a rarity. If you are looking to lose weight, color your dining area blue, which makes food appear unnatural and renders it less palatable.

in a room, while yellow accents suggest summer. Water is defined by light or medium tones of blue or green-blue turquoise, which relate to the free-flowing nature of the substance.

Monochromatic white is calming. When decorating with various values of white in conjunction with its near neighbor beige, a space takes on an oceanside feel, reflecting our nurturing associations with water. The sound of the ocean is always relaxing, and we stimulate the sense of hearing by incorporating colors commonly seen down by the sea. Use natural stone for cocktail and end tables to increase the sense of lounging in the hot sun, bring in unstructured floral arrangements as representative of wild grasses and incorporate beige carpeting to suggest undulating sand dunes. Nurture yourself with color use, then share yourself with friends and family and let the unbroken chain of caring begin.

COLORS FOR SPIRITUALITY

SPIRITUALITY SPIRITUALITY ALITY SPIRITUALITY SPIRITUALITY

OUR LIVES ARE NOT CONFINED TO THE MERELY PHYSICAL. WERE THIS SO, LIFE

WOULD BE EMPTY, DEVOID OF MEANING. FOR MILLIONS THE WORLD OVER, FEEDING

THE SOUL IS A DAILY EXERCISE. IN MANY CULTURES (AND IN MANY PREVIOUS ERAS),

ALLOCATING A SPACE THAT ALLOWS FOR PRAYERFUL THOUGHT IS A NECESSITY

OF LIFE. CREATING IN ITSELF IS AN ACT OF SPIRITUALITY, AND IN DECORATING THE

SACRED SPACE WE PRAY TWICE, MUCH AS THOREAU WARMED HIMSELF TWICE

FIRST BY CHOPPING WOOD, THEN BY BURNING IT.

A SPIRITUAL ENVIRONMENT INCLUDES COLORS THAT RADIATE SUBLIME

QUIETUDE OR ARE HEAVY WITH SYMBOLISM. FOR THE ROOM'S DOMINANT HUE,

CHOOSE MEDIUM TO DARKER VALUES THAT GIVE CALMNESS AND SERENITY, SUCH

AS BROWN OR BLUE. IN MANY FAITHS, CERTAIN COLORS ARE A SHORTHAND FOR

opposite: Alive with the power of the almighty sun and the purple raiment of Menelaus, it's a pagan delight! Worship Apollo or find your own Muse; either way the room is ready for a journey through the past in electric hues suggestive of regality and high intellectual concepts while wed in dynamic complementary fashion.

spiritual communion; orange traditionally suggests the radiation of inner spirit, forest green is contemplative, and red signifies the heart. Colors such as these free your thoughts to meditate on the infinite and start or end your day connected to a higher power.

Perhaps the most obvious spiritual color is white. White has a purifying effect on an environment when it is used in large quantities on walls or represented on special spiritual occasions in decorative objects. White, as the innocence of love, creates a feeling of oneness with the spiritual world. Use symbolic colors as contrast in a white-walled environment to lend a sense of emotional clarity to a room. High contrast will make inspirational objects leap from the surroundings and into the consciousness. For a feeling of the

top: Pure white cleanses the soul as well as the body. When used with healing green, the sense of spiritual healing is increased.

bottom: Overall blue is tranquil, while the orange fish seemingly caught in the fisherman's net, as in New Testament parable, is seen in the shower curtain. The symbol of the fish is often found in Christian philosophy.

opposite: Calming blue soothes the soul in cool tile and wall color. Lie back in the drawn bath and let blue canoe you to a spiritual realm.

sublime, think of the tranquility a stained glass window imparts to a space. Recreate that mood by utilizing sheers or pleated shades as window treatments that tint the air with color, such as serene blue or a gentle pink.

Colors that symbolize uplifting spiritual emotions also tranquilize the soul. Possibilities include gold, which represents the eternal; heavenly blue to help turn thoughts outward; or purple, denoting spiritual passion. Evergreens have long been associated with eternal life, due to their seemingly undying nature. Red brings a feeling of

unity and commonality of cause, while reminding us of the burning spiritual flame within. Crimson walls with gold accent pieces create a serene space that is hushed and quiet. Blue walls are restful, communicating in silence what we cannot say. When combined with the solidity of brown, as in the wood of the forest, the two provide stability and comfort, relaxed in the presence of the infinite, finding a place of respite from the cares of the day.

Green, the spiritual healer, is easily represented in leafy plants placed about your home. Black

top: The color of Lord Krishna, orange is sublime. Reincarnate yourself in temples of the mind. Chant your mantra and do the Hindu, cross-legged on floor pillows and one with the universe. Can you smell the insense?

bottom: The glow of inner knowledge is represented by the clay wall. This is counterpointed with eighteenth-century Rationalism as evidenced in the Hepplewhite-style chairs in gray. John Wesley could methodically cook-up Methodism here.

right: The Romanesque arches on the wall in faux stone finish are reminiscent of early Christian churches. The overall room color combined with the serenity of the bath sedates the mind and the body while cleansing the soul. Note the "Shepard's Crook" motif, an early symbolic Christian metaphor, on the window treatments.

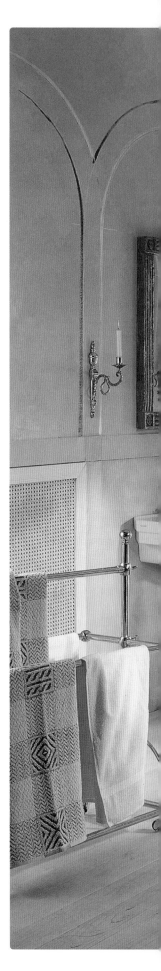

COLOR AND SPACE

The colors you choose will have an impact on the perceived size of your room. Darker shades will seem to make a space contract, while light values make a room expand. Don't fall into the trap of always using color to expand a small space. Try going with the architectural nature of the room, and instead use dark colors to increase the sense of cozy closeness.

following page, left: The Buddha statue begninly oversees the moonswept colors here. The serenity of the Oriental garden at evening, with bathtub as a reflecting pool, brings Siddhartha to your home.

following page, right: These medieval musings are for the Gothic aficionado. The black of the wrought iron as an accent against the casually styled orange window treatments brings to mind the all-pervasive spirituality of the Middle Ages. One expects to hear Gregorian chants echo through the space.

USE LIGHT FOR IMPACT

The light source itself will affect your colors. Florescent light tends toward the blue range, while incandescent light is yellowish. Fluorescents in the kitchen make the hard-surfaced space harder and flattens out colors. Incandescent bulbs are warmer, tending to better highlight colorations.

accents such as wrought iron impart a sense of the past. Black also offers dignified strength and simultaneously suggests both the earth-bound and the limitless universe. Gray is the color of rock, serene in its appearance of solidity. The gray-themed space ties us to tradition, to ancient holy places hewn from stone. Beige can relate to the serenity and spiritual escape of the monk's cell through its unassuming nature.

Lighter values bring happiness, suggesting a world filled with eternal love and peace. These colors create calmness during times of high stress. They bring us hope in the light green of early spring, joy in bright yellow, and innocence in youthful pink. Green is the elysian fields, the color of easy living, far from the worries of winter. The yellow room is alive with the light of a power

greater than ourselves. Pink is our child-like wonder before things boundless and eternal, reminding us that we are perpetually seeking guidance and knowledge. Lilac represents intuition, filling us with a sense of peaceful knowing.

Finally, color is a tool we use to nurture and heal. These two processes are closely associated with the divine, especially when intertwined with creation. Utilizing color to enhance our spiritual well-being is a necessary and inescapable fact of life. We run to it and it answers our prayers, bringing us to life eternal through deep symbolic meaning and by focusing our faith in meditative moments. It reminds us of what life really means and helps us tired travelers find haven. Color is the safe harbor for the ships of our souls.

THE COLOR-CHOICE QUIZ

PINK
TURQUOISE
TURQUOISE BLUE GOLD BLACK BLUE GRAY
PURPLE
GREEN BEIGE GRAY WHITE

We all want to lead better lives. By incorporating the tenets of this book, you can increase certain positive personality traits by regulating the colors you choose for your interiors. While your color preferences are a definite factor in determining the choice of a room's coloration, with *Color Therapy*, the actual function of the colors takes on greater importance. If there is a color that you prefer to decorate a space with, compare it with the chart to be sure it provides the support your life requires.

Choose the emotional, intellectual, and physical traits that you want to emphasize in the space you are decorating from the grid on pages 138–141. For each room in your home, choose the traits that most relate to your perception of what that room should feel like. For each trait you choose, find the color that imparts that quality on the Color Key, located on page 141. Count up how many times each color is chosen. The total will translate the traits you would like the room to possess into color choices. The largest number will indicate the dominant color in the space; the second highest number will give you the secondary color; and the lowest number will suggest the accent color (see "The Rule of 60-30-10" on page 14). If there is a tie between two colors, choose the color that best serves your needs or that you deem as most appropriate for the space.

For example, you may have totals such as ten blue, six red and four yellow. Your answers could translate to 60 percent blue in the room if you desire stability the most. The secondary color could be red if you wish to increase a sense of family ties, again based on your emotional choices from the grid. Yellow would be your accent color if you want the room to be reflective of high skill. If you are decorating a sun room and you want to impart feelings of warmth, vitality, and freshness to the space, your choices will more than likely relate to verdancy (green) and solar energy (yellow). A third example would be perhaps a bedroom in which you want feelings of calmness, quietude, and serenity. Remember to decide on the function of the room before choosing your colors.

Sometimes the color combinations can be unexpected, but don't disregard your results out of hand. When the colors you have chosen don't seem to be a good combination, stop focusing on how the colors go together and instead look at the three selections separately. You may realize that you could use a little more of one of the colors in your life, even if it is only the ten percent value. Some colors, such as turquoise or orange, may surprise you. But if you think about it, you may realize that you already use that color in smaller amounts in your home, and the quiz may just reaffirm the colors you have inadvertently chosen in your life.

If there are certain emotional and psychological aspects of your life that you wish to enhance (perhaps you would like to be more outgoing and verbal), choose the emotional traits you desire from the grid and cross-check them against the Color Key. You can then increase the amount of a particular color in your life to promote these traits.

For example, you may want to increase the amount of blue in your life to help you become a more compassionate, caring individual. You can do this in numerous ways: through your interior design, the clothes you wear, or the car you drive. Your exposure to particular colors and their emotional impact should help you to increase these desirable characteristics of your personality. You can use this tactic in the opposite fashion as well, to eliminate traits you find intrusive, such as anger (decrease red, increase blue) or depression (increase yellow, decrease blue). Have fun!

The Color-Choice Chart

ABSOLUTE	ABUNDANCE	ACCOMMODATING	ACCOUNTABLE	ACTIVE	ADORING
AFFECTION	AFFIRMING	AGREEABLE	AIRY	ALERT	ALIVE
ANALYTICAL	ANCIENT	ANIMATED	APPRECIATIVE	ASSURED	ATTENTION-GETTING
ATTRACTIVE	AUGMENTING	AUTHORITY	BINDING	BLENDING	BLESSED
BRACING	BRAVE	BRIGHT	BRILLIANT	CALM	CAPABLE
CAPTIVATING	CAREFUL	CARING	CASUAL	CAUTIONARY	CHALLENGING
CHARISMATIC	CHEERFUL	CLAIRVOYANT	CLARITY	CLEAN	CLOSE
COMFORTABLE	COMMITMENT	COMPASSIONATE	COMPELLING	CONCENTRATION	CONFIDENT
CONSERVATIVE	CONTENTMENT	CORRECT	COURAGEOUS	COZY	CRAFTY
DEDICATED	DEEP FEELINGS	DEFINITE	DELICATE	DEPENDABLE	DESIRE
DIRECT	DIVINE	DREAMY	DRIFTING	DURABLE	DUTIFUL

DYNAMIC	EAGER	EASY	EFFECTIVE	EGO DRIVEN	EMOTIONAL
EMPOWERING	ENCOURAGING	ENTERPRISING	ENTICING	ESTABLISHED	ETERNAL
EXACT	EXPANSIVE	EXPERTISE	FAITHFUL	FAME	FAMILY TIES
FANTASY	FEMININE	FETCHING	FLEXIBLE	FORCEFUL	FORGIVING
FORMAL	FORTHRIGHT	FRESH	FUN	GEMLIKE	GENIAL
GENEROUS	GENIUS	GIVING	GOAL-ORIENTED	GRACIOUS	GROUNDED
HAPPY	HEALING	HEALTHFUL	HEARTY	HEAT	HEAVENLY
HELPFUL	HIGH REGARD	HIGHER POWER	HIGH SKILL	HONESTY	HONOR
HUMBLE	HUMILITY	HUMOROUS	HYPNOTIZING	IDEAL	IMPORTANCE
IMPOSING	IMPRESSIVE	INFINITE	INNER PEACE	INNOCENCE	INSIGHTFUL
INSTRUCTIONAL	INTELLECTUAL	INTERESTING	INTIMATE	INTROSPECTIVE	INTUITIVE

INVENTIVE	KIND	LASTING	LIGHT	LIQUID	LISTENING
LIVELY	LOVE	MAGICAL	MEANINGFUL	MEDITATIVE	MEMORIES
METHODICAL	MODESTY	MYSTERIOUS	NEUTRAL	NEW THOUGHT	NEWNESS
NOBLE	NONCONFORMITY	NONVERBAL	NOURISHING	OPEN	ORDERLY
OUTDOORSY	OUTGOING	PARTICULAR	PASSIONATE	PEACEFUL	PEOPLE-LOVING
PERCEPTIVE	PERFORMANCE-ENHANCING	PERMANENT	PLAYFUL	PLIABLE	POSITIVE
POTENT	PRECISION	PREPARED	PRESENT TENSE	PRIVATE	PROCEDURAL
PRODUCTIVE	PROFESSIONAL	PROGRESSIVE	PROLIFIC	PROPHETIC	PROSPERITY
PROTEAN	PROTECTING	PROVOCATIVE	PSYCHIC	PURE	QUICK WITTED
QUIET	RANDOMNESS	RARITY	RATIONAL	REASONING	REASSURING
REENERGIZING	REFLECTIVE	REGAL	REGENERATIVE	RELAXING	RELEASING
RESERVED	RESOLUTE	RESOURCEFUL	RESPONSIBLE	RESTFUL	RESTORATIVE

RESTRAINED	REVERENTIAL	RICH	RISK TAKING	ROBUST	ROYAL
SACRIFICE	SANCTUARY	SATISFACTION	SEARCHING	SECURE	SELF-CONTROL
SELF-ESTEEM	SELFLESS	SENSITIVE	SERENITY	SETTLED	SEXUALITY
SHARING	SHELTERING	SINCERE	SKILLFUL	SNUG	SOFTNESS
SOLID	SOLITUDE	SOOTHING	SPECIFIC	SPIRITUAL	SPONTANEOUS
STABLE	STATELY	STEADFAST	STILLNESS	STRENGTH	STRICT
STRONG WILLED	STURDY	SUBLIME	SUN FILLED	SUPPORTIVE	SURRENDER
SUSTAINING	TALKATIVE	TASTEFUL	TEACHABLE	TEMPORAL	THOUGHTFUL
TOUGH	TRADITION	TRANQUIL	TRANSCENDENT	TRANSPARENT	TRUSTING
TRUST INSPIRING	TRUTHFUL	UNDERSTANDING	UNIFYING	UNIQUE	UNITING
UNIVERSALITY	UNORTHODOX	UNPREDICTABLE	UPLIFTING	VERSATILE	VIBRANT
VISIONARY	VITAL	VULNERABLE	WEALTH	WISDOM	WORSHIPFUL

The Color-Choice Key

Beige				
Blending	Enterprising	Genial	Neutral	Randomness
Careful	Enticing	Gracious	New thought	Sharing
Casual	Expansive	Hypnotizing	Pliable	Unifying
Dutiful	Flexible	Modesty	Private	Versatile

Black				
Absolute	Definite	Forthright	Orderly	Reserved
Authority	Established	Infinite	Permanent	Reverential
Calm	Faithful	Lasting	Rational	Specific
Correct	Formal	Noble	Releasing	Tradition

Blue				
Assured	Compassionate	Meditative	Restful	Stable
Capable	Durable	Mysterious	Restrained	Steadfast
Caring	Emotional	Productive	Sensitive	Tasteful
Clarity	Giving	Professional	Solid	Trust inspiring

Brown				
Close	Deep feelings	Kind	Relaxing	Sheltering
Comfortable	Easy	Nonverbal	Resourceful	Snug
Contentment	Encouraging	Protecting	Restorative	Stillness
Cozy	Hearty	Reassuring	Secure	Supportive

Gold				
Binding	Ideal	Meaningful	Rich	Strict
Brilliant	Impressive	Memories	Satisfaction	Vibrant
Conservative	Intimate	Rarity	Self-esteem	Wealth
Desire	Lively	Reflective	Spiritual	Worshipful

Gray				
Accountable	Direct	Introspective	Settled	Strong willed
Bracing	Drifting	Resolute	Skillful	Sturdy
Concentration	High regard	Responsible	Soothing	Tough
Dependable	Imposing	Sanctuary	Stately	Thoughtful

Green				
Abundance	Commitment	Nourishing	Present tense	Quick witted
Agreeable	Healing	Outdoorsy	Prolific	Talkative
Alive	Humility	Outgoing	Prophetic	Teachable
Animated	Humorous	Prepared	Prosperity	

Orange				
Adoring	Cautionary	Healthful	Self-control	Transcendent
Affirming	Fame	Humble	Selfless	Truthful
Alert	Generous	Methodical	Serenity	Understanding
Appreciative	Grounded	Provocative	Sincere	Universality

Pink				
Attractive	Inventive	People loving	Reenergizing	Unique
Expertise	Love	Playful	Softness	Unorthodox
Fantasy	Newness	Precision	Solitude	Unpredictable
Feminine	Nonconformity	Quiet	Tranquil	

Purple				
Compelling	Honor	Passionate	Regal	Uplifting
Forceful	Importance	Positive	Sacrifice	Visionary
Genius	Intuitive	Potent	Searching	Wisdom
Helpful	Magical	Psychic	Sublime	

Red				
Active	Challenging	Effective	Heat	Royal
Analyzing	Confident	Ego driven	Inner peace	Sexuality
Ancient	Courageous	Empowering	Risk taking	Uniting
Brave	Dynamic	Family ties	Robust	

Turquoise					
Augmenting	Eternal	Gem like	Listening	Performance-	Regenerative
Charismatic	Fellowship	Insightful	Motivational	enhancing	Vital
Clairvoyant	Fresh	Interesting	Open	Procedural	
Eager	Fun	Liquid		Progressive	

White				
Accommodating	Delicate	Heavenly	Peaceful	Reasoning
Airy	Dreamy	Instructional	Perceptive	Surrender
Clean	Exact	Light	Protean	Temporal
Dedicated	Forgiving	Particular	Pure	Vulnerable

Yellow				
Attention getting	Cheerful	Goal-oriented	Honesty	Strength
Blessed	Crafty	Happy	Innocence	Sun filled
Bright	Divine	Higher power	Intellectual	Sustaining
Captivating	Fetching	High skill	Spontaneous	Trusting

Bibliography

Blakemore, Colin, ed. *Vision: Coding and Efficiency.* Cambridge: Cambridge University Press, 1999.

Buckley, Mary, ed. *Color Theory: A Guide to Information Sources.* Detroit: Gale Research Company, 1975.

Davidoff, Jules B. *Cognition Through Color.* Cambridge: MIT Press, 1991.

Gage, John. *Color and Meaning: Art, Science, and Symbolism.* Berkeley: University of California Press, 1999.

Garau, Augusto. *Color Harmonies.* Translated by Nicola Bruno. Chicago: University of Chicago Press, 1993.

Gerritsen, Franz. *Theory and Practice of Color: A Color Theory Based on Laws of Perception.* New York: Van Nostrand Reinhold, 1975.

Lüscher, Max. *The Lüscher Color Test.* Translated from the German and edited by Ian A. Scott. New York: Random House, 1969.

Miller, David. *The Wisdom of the Eye.* San Diego: Academic Press, 2000.

Riley, Charles A. *Color Codes: Modern Theories of Color in Philosophy, Painting and Architecture, Literature, Music, and Psychology.* Hanover: University Press of New England, 1995.

Rodiek, Robert W. *The First Steps in Seeing.* Sunderland: Sinauer and Associates, 1998.

Sheppard, Joseph. *Human Color Perception: A Critical Study of the Experimental Foundation.* New York: American Elsevier Publishing Company, 1968.

Teevan, Richard Collier, and Birney, Robert C., eds. *Color Vision: An Enduring Problem in Psychology.* Princeton: Van Nostrand Reinhold, 1961.

Photo Credits

Nick Allen, *Living Etc.*, IPC Syndication, 12, 23, 41 (top square)

Peter Aprahamian, *Living Etc.*, IPC Syndication, 124 (bottom)

Artville Stock Images 37, 57 (bottom), 68

Henry Bourne, 99

Wulf Brackrock, Jahreszeiten Verlag, 87, 128 (bottom), 129

St. Christiansen, Jahreszeiten Verlag, 130

Jonn Coolidge, 52 (top), 88, 127

Chris Craymer, *House and Garden*, Conde Nast Publications, 126

Steve Dalton, *Living Etc.*, IPC Syndication, 30, 53, 76, 77, 92

Jake Fitzjones, *Living Etc.*, IPC Syndication, 110

Winfried Heinze, *Living Etc.*, IPC Syndication, 45, 49, 93 (top), 95

Hayo Heye, Jahreszeiten Verlag, 109

Living Etc., IPC Syndication, 29 (top), 89, 93 (bottom)

Craig Knowles, *Living Etc.*, IPC Syndication, 6 (top square)

Ray Main, Mainstream, 3 (right), 6 (middle square), 9, 12, 13, 14, 17 (bottom square), 20, 21, 22, 25, 28, 31, 33 (top square), 36, 39, 41 (bottom square), 44, 47, 52 (bottom), 58, 59, 60, 61, 63, 66, 67, 69, 70, 71, 72, 73, 74, 75, 78, 79, 86 (top), 90 (top left), 100, 101, 102, 103, 105, 106, 107, 115, 116, 117, 118, 120, 121, 128 (top), 134

J. P. Masclet, *Living Etc.*, IPC Syndication, 84, 91

Barbel Miebach, Jahreszeiten Verlag, 56, 90 (bottom right)

Architektur und Wohnen, Heiner Orth, Jahreszeiten Verlag, 3 (left and middle), 57 (top), 81, 82, 83, 98

Michael Paul, 29 (bottom), 97, 125

Lucy Pope, *Living Etc.*, IPC Syndication, 17 (top square), 104, 119

Sven C. Raben, Jahreszeiten Verlag, 51, 62

Christi Roehl, Jahreszeiten Verlag, 132

Jeanette Schaun, Jahreszeiten Verlag, 131

Tom Stewart, *Living Etc.*, IPC Syndication, 123

Akira Takeda, Photonica, 46 (top)

Kevin Thomas, 6 (bottom square), 10, 18, 26, 33 (bottom square), 34, 42, 85, 86 (bottom), 114 (top)

Helge Tundt, Jahreszeiten Verlag, 96

Verity Welstead, *Living Etc.*, IPC Syndication, 54, 65, 112, 114 (bottom), 124 (top)

Simon Whitmore, *Living Etc.*, IPC Syndication, 46 (bottom), 135

Mark McCauley, ASID, is a professional member of the American Society of Interior Designers. He is a former nationally syndicated columnist for the *Chicago Sun-Times* and senior interior designer for Marshall Fields, Chicago. Mr. McCauley is the founder and served as the first editor-in-chief of *Fine Furniture International* Magazine, to which he still contributes regularly. Mr. McCauley has spoken to audiences around the country on interior design philosophy and has made numerous appearances on HGTV. He is currently regional design director for Plunkett's Furniture in Chicago, Illinois and writes the column "Look Alikes" for the *Chicago Tribune Home and Garden* section. Mr. McCauley resides in the Chicago area with his wife Diana and two sons, Stephan and Christopher. He can be reached by e-mail at ColorTherapy@aol.com.

The Author

Dedication

In loving memory of my father Dr. John McCauley, Ph.D. and with my mother Mary's constant faith.

For my wife Diana and my two precious sons, Stephan and Christopher. I am yours.

To John and Mary Robnett, Jack and Theresa, Max and Abby, thanks for everything!

To my sister Mary, my "big brothers" Denis and Edward McCauley, my Aunt Loretta, my Aunt Olive Ann, and all my many cousins who shared childhood dreams with me: Thank you for loving me.

Special thanks to Martin Engblom, S.A. and Dr. Edward Mascorro for their invaluable assistance.

Dunka Martha, ditto Jaybird! Oh, Susannah!

And, of course, where would any of us be without "The Cuddler"?

Mark